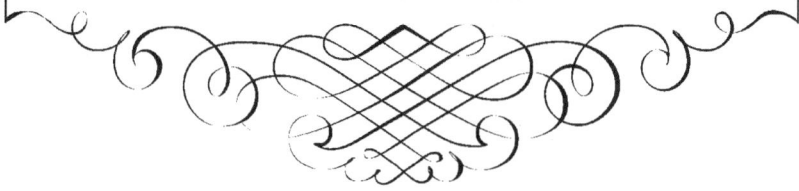

ISBN 978-1-333-77483-7
PIBN 10546502

For support please visit www.forgottenbooks.com

English
Français
Deutsche
Italiano
Español
Português

www.forgottenbooks.com

Mythology Photography **Fiction**
Fishing Christianity **Art** Cooking
Essays Buddhism Freemasonry
Medicine **Biology** Music **Ancient
Egypt** Evolution Carpentry Physics
Dance Geology **Mathematics** Fitness
Shakespeare **Folklore** Yoga Marketing
Confidence Immortality Biographies
Poetry **Psychology** Witchcraft
Electronics Chemistry History **Law**
Accounting **Philosophy** Anthropology
Alchemy Drama Quantum Mechanics
Atheism Sexual Health **Ancient History**
Entrepreneurship Languages Sport
Paleontology Needlework Islam
Metaphysics Investment Archaeology
Parenting Statistics Criminology
Motivational

ILLEGALITY

OF THE

TRIAL

OF

JOHN W. WEBSTER

BY LYSANDER SPOONER.

BOSTON:
PUBLISHED BY BELA MARSH, 25 CORNHILL.
SOLD ALSO BY REDDING AND COMPANY, HOTCHKISS AND COMPANY, AND
FETTRIDGE AND COMPANY, BOSTON.
1850.

ILLEGALITY

OF THE

TRIAL

OF

JOHN W. WEBSTER.

BY LYSANDER SPOONER.

BOSTON:

BELA MARSH, 25 CORNHILL.

1850.

Wright's Steam Press, 3 Water st.

ARGUMENT.

Dr. Webster was not tried by a legal jury; but by a jury *packed*, by the court, either with a view to a more easy conviction than could otherwise be obtained, or with a view to a conviction which otherwise could not be obtained at all.

The jury was packed by excluding from the panel three persons, on account of their opposition to capital punishment, and substituting in their stead three persons not thus opposed. That opposition, it was supposed by the court, (and correctly too, of course), would either render the persons entertaining it less ready to convict the defendant, than they otherwise would be; or would prevent them from convicting at all, whatever the evidence might be.

But exclusion for either or both of these reasons is illegal. If the punishment prescribed by statute, be such as to disincline, or deter, the minds or consciences of the men drawn as jurors, from a conviction, the statute must fail of execution, rather than the jury be packed to avoid that obstacle.

Even if the persons, drawn as jurors, should themselves request to be excused from serving, *or should even refuse to be sworn*, on the ground that they could not conscientiously render a verdict " according to the evidence," if that verdict were to be followed by the penalty of death, *still the court could not discharge them.* The trial must, in the first place, be postponed until a subsequent term of the court, and until an entire new jury be drawn. If this new jury should have among them persons entertaining the same scruples, as those drawn at the former term, the trial must be again postponed; and so on, from term to term, until a jury, drawn in the usual way, shall be found, who will consent to be sworn to try the case. If such a jury cannot be obtained at all, then the trial must be postponed until the statute, prescribing the punishment of death, be repealed, and such a penalty substituted, as jurors will *all* consent to aid in enforcing. In no event, and for no reason whatever, can the jury be packed, in the manner it was done in Dr. Webster's case, *for that is destroying the trial by jury itself*,—as I will now proceed to show.

The trial by jury is a trial by " *the country*," in contradistinction to a trial by *the government*. The jurors are drawn by lot from the mass of the people, for the very purpose of having all classes of minds and feelings, that prevail among the people at large, represented in the jury. They are drawn by lot from the mass of the people, for the very purpose of making the jury a fair epitome, mentally and morally, of " the country,"—that is, of the *whole* country.

A tribunal, thus selected, is supposed to be a more just, impartial, and competent tribunal, than the government itself, or any department of it would be. And unanimity, on the part of the members of this tribunal, is required, in order that no man may be punished or condemned, unless the whole country, (so far as that is supposed to be fairly represented by the jury), shall concur in the conviction and punishment. This concurrence of the *whole* " country," as a condition of conviction and punishment, is required from motives of both justice and caution towards the life, liberty, property, and character of the person accused. It is supposed that if *any portion* of " the country," (as represented in the jury), dissent from the conviction or punishment, that dissent gives sufficient reason at least to *doubt* the propriety or justice of such conviction or punishment.

Now it is clear, that if the government can exclude, on account either of their opinions or feelings, any persons thus drawn by lot, the trial is no longer a trial by " the country," but only by a portion of the country. It is, in fact, a trial by *the government*, instead of " *the country*,"—because it is a trial by that portion only of the country, which has been selected by the government, on account of their having no opinions or feelings different from its own.

Such an exclusion, therefore, works the abolition of the trial by jury itself,—because it works the abolition of the trial by " *the country*," and institutes a trial by *the government*,—or, what is the same thing, a trial by persons selected by the government, on account of their concurrence in, or their subservience to, its own opinions and feelings.

Whenever, therefore, the government presumes even to question the persons drawn as jurors, as to whether they entertain any opinions or feelings different from those entertained by the government, (as the latter are expressed in the statute book), and says to one "be sworn," and to another "stand aside," (according as he concurs with, or dissents from, the opinions or feelings of the government), the government manifestly assumes to abolish the trial "by the country," and to institute a new tribunal, constituted solely of persons specially selected by the government, on account of their readiness to carry out the purposes of the government.

But it will be said that the difference of opinion, between the government and the individual—(which constitutes the ground, on which the former excludes the latter from the panel)—is a difference about that, with which the juror has nothing to do, to wit, the punishment, and not the guilt, of the accused person.

There are two answers to this objection :

1. The conviction is sought—or rather the guilt or innocence of the accused person is sought to be ascertained—mainly, if not solely, with a view to his punishment, if he be found guilty. Punishment, or no punishment, then, is the *practical* question at issue. Conviction is but a means, punishment the end. The former has reference, wholly, or nearly so, to the latter. Now, it is to be observed that, in law, means are rarely considered independently of ends. They are never authorized, independently of ends. The difference between them, then, is theoretical, rather than practical. Although, therefore, there may be a theoretical distinction between the question of conviction, and the question of punishment, there can hardly be said to be any *practical*, or even *legal*, difference between them.

2. Admitting, for the sake of the argument, a clear legal distinction between the question of guilt, and the question of punishment, it does not follow that the former is to be determined without any reference to the latter. The law does not require a man to cease to be a man, and act without regard to consequences, when he becomes a juror. The courts themselves, at the same time that they exclude one man from the panel because he looks forward to the consequences of a conviction, will yet instruct those who remain on the panel, that they are to scrutinize the testimony with all that caution which the momentous results of their decision naturally dictate. No court presumes to tell a jury that they are to try a capital case with the same indifference and unconcern as to consequences, that they would a case where the results of their decision would be less important. On the contrary, all courts usually press upon a jury a solemn consideration of the consequences involved, as a motive to the exercise of unusual, and even extreme, caution. . But in so doing, it is plain that they act upon an entirely opposite principle from that on which they acted in excluding individuals from the panel. Because these latter individuals looked forward to the consequences of their decision, and felt a little more sensibility to those consequences than the statute requires, or the government approves, the government excludes them ; while, at the same time, the government instructs those who remain on the panel, that they are to keep these consequences in view, and act with corresponding caution.

The result, therefore, is, that the government—

when it affixes the penalty of death to the commission of a crime, and excludes a man from the panel on account of his views of that penalty—virtually assumes to set up a standard of sensibility, in regard to the matter in issue, beyond which a juror may not go. And the consequence is, that the accused person is tried, not by " the country "—not by persons who fairly represent all the degrees of sensibility, which prevail among the people at large —but by persons selected by the government for no other reason than that they lack that degree of sensibility, touching the matter in issue, which a greater or less portion of " the country " possess. To select a jury on this principle, is nothing more nor less than *packing* a jury,—in the worst sense of that term. What is ever the object of packing a jury, but to get rid of all persons, whose sensibilities will be likely to thwart the purposes of the government ? that is, defeat (or secure, as the case may be) the conviction and punishment of the accused, contrary to the wishes of the government ?

The provision of the Bill of Rights, which guarantees to every man a trial by " the country," does not say that he shall be tried by such portions only of the country as possess but a *statutory* degree of sensibility—a degree of sensibility not incompatible with the efficiency of such penal codes as may be enacted by the legislature—but by " the country " *unreservedly*—by " the country " with all its sensibilities. And if it happen that those sensibilities are such as that any persons, drawn as jurors, either will not try, or will not convict, where death is the penalty to follow, then the statute affixing that penalty must be so changed as to conform to the sensibilities of the country, or it must become a dead letter, and criminals go unpunished, and even untried, rather than the trial "by the country" be abolished, and a trial by the government be substituted. Otherwise the statute prevails over the Bill of Rights.

Whenever the statute, that affixes the penalty, and the Bill of Rights, which guarantees a trial " by the country," are found to be *practically* incompatible with each other, the latter, being the paramount law, must prevail. But the government, by excluding a part of " the country " from the panel, in order that the statute may have effect, virtually say that the statute must prevail over the Bill of Rights.

It may here be mentioned, in passing, that it seems never to have occurred to the government, that if they assume to set up a statutory standard of sensibility for jurors, and to exclude from the panel all men, whose sensibilities rise above that standard, they ought to be equally bound to exclude all whose sensibilities fall below it. But they make no inquisition in that direction.

But, in truth, opposition to capital punishment does not *necessarily* imply any unusual degree of sensibility. It may result solely from the conviction—founded on the incontestible experience of mankind—that there is no such certainty in human testimony, as to secure the innocent from suffering the penalty designed only for the guilty. In multitudes of cases, where the accused were innocent, the evidence has nevertheless been so strong as to justify, and even to require, a conviction, if the principle be admitted that human testimony is, *in its nature*, sufficiently certain to justify or require a conviction, that is to be followed by the penalty of death. A person, therefore, may be opposed to capital punishment for this reason alone—a reason that implies a deliberate and philosophical estimate of the weight of human testimony. Yet, all those, who thus weigh the evidence a little more philosophically, and in the light of a wider observation, than the government, must be excluded. Is such a principle to be tolerated ? One of the very objects of the trial by jury, is to have the evidence weighed differently from what it is supposed the government might weigh it. Yet now, because a man thus weighs it, he is excluded from the panel.

Again. It is not only a supposable case, but a highly probable one, that a person may be opposed to the death penalty, on the ground that it is a "*cruel* punishment," (and if unnecessary, it is " cruel,") and that therefore the government has no *constitutional* right to inflict it—" cruel punishments " being expressly prohibited by the Bill of Rights. In that case a man would be excluded from the panel simply for forming a different opinion from the government, on a question as to the constitutional powers of the government. If such a principle prevail, all barriers, interposed by a jury, not only to the infliction of " cruel punishments," but to the assumption, by the government, of all manner of unconstitutional authority, are swept away.

The question has thus far been discussed on the

supposition that the question of punishment, and the question of guilt, are distinct—and that, *in strict law*, the jury are judges only of the latter. And I take it for granted that it has been shown, that even under that supposition, men cannot be excluded from the panel by the government, in order that the will of the government, (as expressed in its criminal code), may escape the influence and the veto of that moral law, and that law of human nature, which require and compel all men, jurors as well as others, to regard more or less the consequences that are to follow their actions. If the criminal code be *practically* inconsistent with that law of human nature, and theoretically inconsistent with the moral law, as this is understood by any considerable portion of "the country," the code must give way to, or be made to conform to, those higher laws, or the "trial by the country" must be abandoned.

But, in fact, the position is not a true one, that the jury have legally nothing to do with the question of punishment, but only with the question of guilt. The language of Magna Charta is equally explicit on the point of punishment, as on that of conviction; and it provides as clearly that a man shall not be *punished*, but by "the judgment of his peers," as that he shall not be condemned but by the same "judgment." These are the words of Magna Charta:

"No freeman shall be arrested, or imprisoned, or deprived of his freehold, or his liberties, or free customs, or be outlawed, or exiled, or in any manner destroyed; *nor* will we pass upon him, nor condemn him, unless by the legal judgment of his peers, or the law of the land." *

Here are plainly two clauses in this chapter of Magna Charta—two distinct provisions. The first relates to the arrest and punishment, the other to the conviction. That they are distinct clauses, is proved by the fact that they are separated from each other by the disjunctive " *nor.*" Thus, " No freeman shall be arrested, imprisoned, or deprived of his freehold, or his liberties, or free customs, or be outlawed, or exiled, or in any manner destroyed ;" (all the preceding words are but saying that no freeman shall be arrested or *punished;*) " *nor* will we pass upon him, nor condemn him, but by the judgment of his peers, or the law of the land."

It is plain that " the judgment of his peers " goes to the whole question, and to the *separate* questions, of *punishment* and guilt.

And this is as it should be. The trial by jury was intended to be—what it has so often been denominated—" the palladium of liberty;" the great bulwark for the protection of individuals against the oppression of the government. But it would be but a partial and imperfect protection against that oppression, if the " judgment " of the jury, as to the degree of punishment to be inflicted, could not be interposed between the convict and the govern-

---

* The phrase, " *By the law of the land,*" (say Coke, Kent, Story, and others,) does not mean a statute passed by a legislature—(for then this clause would impose no restraint upon the Legislature)—but is a technical phrase, meaning, " by the due course and process of law," which Coke afterwards explains to be, " by indictment or presentment of good and lawful men, where such deeds be done, in due manner, or by writ original of the common law," &c. &c. 2 Coke's Institutes, 45, 50 ; 2 Kent's Comm. 13 ; 3 Story's Comm. 661 ; 4 Hill's Rep. 146 : **19** Wendell, 676 ; 4 Dev. N. C. Rep. 15.

ment. The government could punish the slightest offences in the most cruel and unreasonable manner. The people, as single individuals, need protection against cruel and unreasonable punishments, as well as against unjust condemnations. And they can secure this protection only on the principles here contended for.

If there could be any doubt as to the meaning of the language of Magna Charta, on this point, that doubt would be settled by an established rule of interpretation, which courts are bound to apply to all laws and legal instruments whatsoever, viz., that we are to get as much good out of a law, (or other legal instrument,) as possible; that is, that we are to make its words mean as much good, (in connexion with the matter of which they are treating,) as they can fairly be made to mean. Interpreted by this rule, this chapter of Magna Charta is explicit beyond cavil, to the point that the "judgment" of the jury shall be had on the question of punishment, as well as on the question of guilt.

The *spirit* of the provision undoubtedly requires that "the judgment" of the jury shall be taken on the question of punishment *separately* from the question of guilt. But where a juror, knowing the extent of the punishment authorized by the statute, consents to try a case, and renders his verdict without offering any objection to that punishment, his consent to it may, *perhaps*, be fairly inferred. But where he refuses to try the case, solely because he disapproves of such punishment, his consent is clearly withheld.

The Bill of Rights of Massachusetts, is, if possible, more explicit than Magna Charta in submitting the question of *punishment* to the "judgment" of the jury; indeed, the first clause on the subject, *in terms*, makes the whole trial, (so far as the jury are concerned,) a question of punishment, rather than of guilt. That clause, it will be seen, uses no terms that express conviction of guilt, as a separate thing from punishment. It does not say, like Magna Charta, that no man shall be "passed upon, nor condemned;" it only says that no subject shall be arrested or *punished*. It is only in the second paragraph that the trial of his guilt by a jury is *clearly* provided for.

These are the words:

"No subject shall be arrested, imprisoned, despoiled or deprived of his property, immunities, or privileges, put out of the protection of the law, exiled, or deprived of his life, liberty, or estate, but by the judgment of his peers, or the law of the land.

"And the government shall not make any law that shall subject any person to a capital or infamous punishment, except for the government of the army and navy, without trial by jury."

The language of the first of these paragraphs seems to be explicit, that the jury are to pass upon the question of punishment, and I take it for granted that it settles the question.*

---

* Because the jury pass upon the question of punishment, it must not be supposed, if they award any particular punishment, or degree of punishment, that their decision is necessarily final, any more than that their verdict that he is guilty is necessarily final. A man may be relieved of the punishment by the executive, or acquitted of the guilt by the judiciary, (on a question of law being

To conclude. It is plain, that if the more humane and conscientious persons can be discharged from the panel, on account of their revolting against the barbarity of the laws, which they are called upon to aid in enforcing, an accused person does not have a trial by "the country," but only by the more inhuman and unfeeling portion of it.

Suppose the statute were to prescribe the penalty of death for a theft of forty shillings, (as it has sometimes done in England.) Probably not one man in ten in this Commonwealth would consent to be sworn to try a person accused of such a theft. In such a case, could all the men who were thus scrupulous, be excluded from the panel, or even be discharged at their own request, until a jury were packed entirely of men so brutal as to be willing to have a man hanged for stealing forty shillings? Certainly not, I think. And if not, then men cannot be discharged at all, on account of their opposition to such penalties as may be prescribed by statute ; and whenever men, drawn as jurors, refuse to be sworn to try a case, on account of the penalty annexed to the offence to be tried, the trial must, in the first instance, be postponed until, at some subsequent term of the court, a jury drawn in the usual way, shall be found, who will swear to try the case. If such a jury can never be found, the trial must stop, until that penalty be changed for

---

raised,) notwithstanding the "judgment" of the jury. But he cannot be convicted of the guilt, nor subjected to the punishment, *against their judgment.* Their judgment is indispensable to his conviction and punishment; but it is not indispensable to his acquittal and discharge. Thus, if their judgment be in *his favor*, it is final; the government cannot appeal from it; but if it be *against him*, he may appeal to the judiciary on the question of guilt, and to the executive, (and to the judiciary also, if the legislature so provide,) on the question of punishment.

such a one as *all men*, drawn as jurors, can conscientiously assent to.

If the doctrine here attempted to be maintained be correct, the trial by jury secures a merciful criminal code—such a code as " the country," (as represented in a jury drawn by lot from the great body of the people,) can conscientiously aid in enforcing. If the doctrine be erroneous, we have no such security. We can have only such a code as a bare majority of the people may chance to approve ; and all that justice and tenderness towards life, liberty, property, and character, which has heretofore forbidden the condemnation of an accused person, so long as any portion of the " country," (as represented in a jury drawn by lot,) doubted his guilt, or disapproved his punishment, must give place to a sternness, not to say ferocity, which packs a jury with a special view to a more easy conviction, or a heavier penalty, than could otherwise be obtained or inflicted.

In Dr. Webster's case, three persons, equal to one fourth of the jury, were excluded from the panel, on account of their opposition to the death penalty. These three persons, it is fair to presume, represented a corresponding portion of the community, that is, one fourth of the whole. Thus one fourth of " the country " were virtually disfranchised of their constitutional right to be heard, both on the question of the guilt, and the question of the punishment, of one of their fellow men. Will so large a portion of the community acquiesce in such a disfranchisement ?

CPSIA information can be obtained
at www.ICGtesting.com
Printed in the USA
BVHW041143150119
537878BV00020B/1179/P

9 781333 774837